GREAT GARLIC RECIPES

APPETIZERS

Roasted ■ Eggplant Dip ■

2 eggplants (about 1 pound
 each)
3 tablespoons sesame tahini*
¼ cup lemon juice
4 cloves garlic, minced
2 teaspoons hot pepper sauce
½ teaspoon salt
 Paprika
1 tablespoon chopped fresh
 parsley

*Available in the ethnic section of the
supermarket or in Middle Eastern grocery
stores.*

1. Prick eggplants in several places
with fork. To roast over charcoal,
place eggplants on grill over hot
coals; cook about 30 to 40 minutes
or until skin is black and blistered
and pulp is soft, turning often. To
roast in oven, preheat oven to
450°F. Place eggplants on baking
sheet; bake about 30 to 40 minutes
or until skin is blistered and pulp is
soft.

2. Peel eggplants when cool enough
to handle. Let cool to room
temperature.

3. Place eggplant pulp in food
processor with tahini, lemon juice,
garlic, hot pepper sauce and salt;
process until smooth. Refrigerate at
least 1 hour before serving to allow
flavors to blend. Sprinkle dip with
paprika and parsley; serve with pita
bread wedges. Garnish with red
chili pepper slices, if desired.

Makes 8 servings

Roasted Eggplant Dip

Herbed Garlic
■ Cheese Spread ■

1 cup (8 ounces) low-fat or
   non-fat cottage cheese
¼ cup roasted garlic (page 7)
1 cup (4 ounces) shredded
   JARLSBERG Cheese or
   JARLSBERG LITE™
   Cheese
½ teaspoon dried tarragon
¼ teaspoon freshly ground
   black pepper

Place cottage cheese in blender
with roasted garlic and blend well.
Add Jarlsberg and tarragon. Blend,
scraping down sides (mixture will
be slightly lumpy). Add pepper; stir
and taste. Add more pepper, if
desired. Serve with carrot or
zucchini rounds, red pepper strips
and celery sticks.

Makes 1½ cups

Note: Spread may be served warm.
Microwave on high 1½ minutes,
stirring every 30 seconds or cook in
double boiler, stirring over
simmering water until warm.

Marshall's Garlic
■ Popcorn ■

10 to 12 cloves garlic, thinly
   sliced
 4 to 5 tablespoons vegetable
   oil
½ cup NEWMAN'S OWN®
   Oldstyle Picture Show
   Popcorn
 1 tablespoon butter
   Garlic salt
   Parmesan cheese (optional)

Rub garlic slices over bottom of an
electric (oil) corn popper. Cook
and stir garlic slices with oil in
small skillet until golden brown.
Drain to remove the garlic slices,
reserving oil and garlic separately.
Pour the oil into the corn popper.
Add NEWMAN'S OWN® Oldstyle
Picture Show Popcorn and pop as
usual. Melt butter; combine with
reserved garlic. After the popping is
completed, place popcorn in
serving bowl. Toss with garlic
butter; season with garlic salt and
Parmesan cheese, if desired.

Makes 4 servings

■ Garlic Bites ■

½ of 16-ounce package frozen
   phyllo dough, thawed to
   room temperature
¾ cup butter, melted
3 large heads garlic, separated
   into cloves, peeled
½ cup finely chopped walnuts
1 cup Italian-style bread
   crumbs

Preheat oven to 350°F. Remove
phyllo from package; unroll and
place on large sheet of waxed
paper. Cut phyllo crosswise into
2-inch-wide strips. Cover phyllo
with large sheet of plastic wrap and
damp, clean kitchen towel. (Phyllo
dries out quickly if not covered.)

Lay 1 strip of phyllo at a time on
flat surface and brush immediately
with melted butter. Place 1 clove of
garlic at end. Sprinkle 1 teaspoon
walnuts along length of strip.

Roll up garlic clove and walnuts in
strip, tucking in side edges as you
roll. Brush Garlic Bite with more
butter. Roll in bread crumbs.
Repeat with remaining phyllo,
garlic, walnuts and butter.

Place Garlic Bites on rack in
shallow roasting pan. Bake 20
minutes.

Makes 24 to 27 appetizers

Garlic Bites

■ Garlic Fritters ■

10 large cloves CHRISTOPHER
    RANCH Fresh Garlic,
    finely chopped
¼ teaspoon salt
1 cup water
6 tablespoons butter
1 cup all-purpose flour
4 eggs
    Oil for deep-frying
¼ cup sour cream
¼ cup grated Parmesan cheese
2 cloves CHRISTOPHER
    RANCH Fresh Garlic,
    minced
2 teaspoons chopped fresh
    tarragon *or* 1 teaspoon
    dried tarragon

Combine finely chopped garlic and salt in small bowl; mash into a paste. Combine water, garlic paste and butter in saucepan over medium heat; bring to a boil. Add flour, stirring quickly into a mass. Remove from heat. Add eggs, 1 at a time, being certain to fully incorporate each one. Form dough into small bite-sized mounds and deep-fry at about 370°F until golden brown. Drain on paper towels. Cut each fritter in half. Combine sour cream, Parmesan, minced garlic and tarragon in small bowl. Spread ½ teaspoon of sour cream mixture on half of each fritter; top with other half. *Makes 4 dozen appetizers*

Roasted Garlic ■ Hummus ■

1 can (15 ounces) chick-peas,
    rinsed and drained
¼ cup fresh parsley, stems
    removed
2 tablespoons roasted garlic
    (page 279)
2 tablespoons lemon juice
2 tablespoons water
½ teaspoon curry powder
3 drops dark sesame oil
    Dash hot pepper sauce

Place chick-peas, parsley, roasted garlic, lemon juice, water, curry powder, sesame oil and hot pepper sauce in food processor or blender; process until smooth, scraping down side of bowl once. Serve with pita bread triangles or crackers.
Makes 6 servings

Fiery Garlic ■ Bagel Thins ■

5 bagels
½ cup (1 stick) butter
6 cloves garlic, minced
2 tablespoons lemon juice
½ teaspoon TABASCO® brand
    Pepper Sauce
    Salt to taste

Preheat broiler. Slice bagels crosswise into fifths. Melt butter in a small saucepan. Add garlic; cook over low heat for 2 minutes or until garlic has softened. Add lemon juice, TABASCO® Sauce and salt to taste. Liberally brush one side of each bagel slice with lemon-garlic butter. Broil bagels on one side until golden. Watch carefully; this only takes a minute. Turn bagels over and broil until golden. Serve hot or store in an airtight container.

Makes 25 bagel thins

■ Salsa Cruda ■

1 cup chopped tomato
2 tablespoons minced onion
2 tablespoons minced fresh cilantro
2 tablespoons lime juice
½ jalapeño pepper,* seeded and minced
3 cloves garlic, minced

Jalapeño peppers can sting and irritate the skin; wear rubber gloves when handling peppers and do not touch eyes. Wash hands after handling.

Combine all ingredients in small bowl; mix well. Serve with tortilla chips.

Makes 4 servings

■ Stuffed Mushrooms ■

12 large mushrooms
2 tablespoons butter or margarine
3 cloves CHRISTOPHER RANCH Elephant Garlic, chopped
3 shallots, chopped
⅔ cup shredded Swiss cheese
⅓ cup dry bread crumbs
Parmesan cheese for garnish

Remove stems from mushrooms; chop stems and reserve caps. Melt butter in medium skillet over medium heat. Add chopped mushroom stems, garlic and shallots; cook and stir until garlic and shallots are soft. Remove from heat; stir in Swiss cheese and bread crumbs. Stuff the mushroom caps full and place in baking dish. Bake in a 375°F oven for 15 to 20 minutes. Sprinkle each with Parmesan before serving.

Makes 4 to 6 servings

■ Venezuelan Salsa ■

1 carrot, finely chopped
1 small onion, finely chopped
1 rib celery, finely chopped
1 mango, peeled, pitted and diced
½ medium papaya, peeled, seeded and diced
½ medium avocado, peeled, pitted and diced
  Juice of 1 lemon
3 cloves garlic, minced
1 jalapeño pepper,* finely chopped
1½ teaspoons ground cumin
½ teaspoon salt
2 tablespoons chopped cilantro

Jalapeño peppers can sting and irritate the skin; wear rubber gloves when handling peppers and do not touch eyes. Wash hands after handling.

Combine all ingredients in medium bowl. Refrigerate several hours to allow flavors to blend. Serve with tortilla chips, carrot and celery sticks or apple wedges.
    Makes 10 servings (¼ cup each)

■ Elephant in a Bowl ■

1 package (8 ounces) cream cheese, softened
1 cup shredded Monterey Jack or Swiss cheese
¼ cup diced mild green chilies
3 cloves CHRISTOPHER RANCH Elephant Garlic, finely chopped
2 tablespoons finely chopped fresh parsley
  Pinch of white pepper
1 large round French bread loaf

Preheat oven to 350°F. Combine cream cheese, Monterey Jack, chilies, garlic, parsley and white pepper in large bowl; blend well. Slice off top of French bread and scoop out enough bread to create a bowl to comfortably hold cheese mixture. Place cheese mixture into bread bowl and replace top. Wrap in foil; bake for 20 to 30 minutes or until heated through. Serve with crackers or French bread slices.
    Makes 8 to 10 servings

Venezuelan Salsa

SOUPS & SALADS

Sweet Pepper Garlic
■ Soup ■

2 teaspoons olive oil
½ cup chopped onion
6 cloves garlic, chopped
3½ cups chicken broth
1 cup cubed potato, unpeeled
1 cup chopped red bell
    pepper
1 cup cottage cheese
2 tablespoons plain yogurt
⅛ teaspoon black pepper

1. Heat oil in medium saucepan over medium heat; add onion and garlic. Cook and stir 3 minutes or until onion is tender. Add chicken broth, potato and bell pepper. Bring to a boil; reduce heat and simmer 10 to 15 minutes or until potato is easily pierced when tested with fork. Remove from heat; cool completely.

2. Place broth mixture in food processor or blender; process until smooth. Refrigerate until completely cool.

3. Place cottage cheese and yogurt in food processor or blender; process until smooth. Set aside ¼ cup cheese mixture. Stir remaining cheese mixture into chilled broth mixture until well blended. Add black pepper; stir well. Top with reserved cheese mixture. Garnish with parsley and bell pepper strips, if desired.

Makes 6 servings

Sweet Pepper Garlic Soup

Albacore Salad Puttanesca with Garlic ■ Vinaigrette ■

2 cups cooked, chilled angel hair pasta
2 cups chopped, peeled plum tomatoes
1 can (4¼ ounces) chopped black olives, drained
1 cup Garlic Vinaigrette Dressing (recipe follows)
1 can (6 ounces) STARKIST® Solid White Tuna, drained and flaked
¼ cup chopped fresh basil leaves

In large bowl, combine chilled pasta, tomatoes, olives and Garlic Vinaigrette Dressing. Add tuna and basil leaves; toss. Serve immediately.   *Makes 2 servings*

Garlic Vinaigrette Dressing

⅓ cup red wine vinegar
2 tablespoons lemon juice
1 to 2 cloves garlic, minced or pressed
1 teaspoon black pepper
Salt
1 cup olive oil

In small bowl, whisk together vinegar, lemon juice, garlic, pepper and salt to taste. Slowly add oil, whisking continuously, until well blended.   *Makes about 1⅓ cups*

Mexican Tortilla ■ Soup ■

1 tablespoon vegetable oil
1 rib celery, sliced
½ cup sliced carrots
3 green onions, sliced
4 cloves garlic, minced
2 cans (about 14 ounces each) chicken broth
⅓ to ½ cup lime juice
½ cup chopped tomato
½ small avocado, chopped
¼ cup chopped seeded cucumber
2 tablespoons finely chopped fresh cilantro, tortilla chips, crushed

Heat oil in medium saucepan over medium heat. Add celery, carrots, green onions and garlic; cook and stir about 5 minutes or until tender. Add chicken broth and lime juice; bring to a boil over high heat. Reduce heat to low; simmer, covered, 15 minutes.

Ladle soup into 4 bowls; divide tomato, avocado and cucumber among bowls. Sprinkle with cilantro and tortilla chips. Serve immediately.   *Makes 4 servings*

Albacore Salad Puttanesca with Garlic Vinaigrette

Layered Mexican ■ Salad ■

1 small head romaine lettuce
Salsa Cruda (page 167)
1 can (15 ounces) black turtle
   beans, rinsed and drained
1 cup frozen corn, thawed and
   drained
1 large cucumber, peeled
1 can (2¼ ounces) sliced
   black olives, drained
1 large lemon
¾ cup mayonnaise
3 tablespoons plain yogurt
4 cloves garlic, minced
½ cup (2 ounces) shredded
   Cheddar cheese
1 green onion, thinly sliced

1. Cut romaine leaves crosswise into ½-inch strips; place half in large serving bowl. Layer with Salsa Cruda, beans and corn.

2. Halve cucumber lengthwise; scoop out and discard seeds. Slice thinly. Place cucumber over corn, sprinkle with olives and top with remaining lettuce.

3. Grate lemon peel; combine with mayonnaise, yogurt and garlic. Juice lemon; stir 3 to 4 tablespoons juice into dressing. Spread dressing evenly over top of salad. Sprinkle with cheese and green onion. Cover; refrigerate 2 hours or up to 1 day.

Makes 12 servings

■ Far East Tabbouleh ■

¾ cup uncooked bulgur
2 tablespoons teriyaki sauce
2 tablespoons lemon juice
1 tablespoon olive oil
¾ cup diced seeded cucumber
¾ cup diced seeded tomato
½ cup thinly sliced green
   onions
½ cup minced fresh cilantro or
   fresh parsley
1 tablespoon minced fresh
   ginger
4 cloves garlic, crushed

1. Combine bulgur and 1¾ cups boiling water in small bowl. Cover with plastic wrap; let stand 45 minutes or until bulgur is puffed, stirring occasionally. Drain in wire mesh sieve; discard liquid.

2. Combine bulgur, teriyaki sauce, lemon juice and oil in large bowl. Stir in cucumber, tomato, onions, cilantro, ginger and garlic until well blended. Cover; refrigerate 4 hours, stirring occasionally.

Makes 4 servings

Layered Mexican Salad

■ Chili Verde ■

½ to ¾ pound boneless lean pork, cut into 1-inch cubes
1 large onion, halved and thinly sliced
6 cloves garlic, chopped or sliced
1 pound fresh tomatillos
1 can (about 14 ounces) chicken broth
1 can (4 ounces) diced mild green chilies
1 teaspoon ground cumin
1½ cups cooked navy or Great Northern beans *or* 1 can (15 ounces) Great Northern beans, rinsed and drained
½ cup lightly packed fresh cilantro, chopped
Sour cream

1. Place pork, onion, garlic and ½ cup water into large saucepan. Cover; simmer over medium-low heat 30 minutes, stirring occasionally (add more water if necessary). Uncover; boil over medium-high heat until liquid evaporates and meat browns.

2. Stir in tomatillos and broth. Cover; simmer over medium heat 20 minutes or until tomatillos are tender. Tear tomatillos apart with 2 forks. Add chilies and cumin.

3. Cover; simmer over medium-low heat 45 minutes or until meat is tender and tears apart easily. (Add more water or broth to keep liquid level the same.) Add beans; simmer 10 minutes or until heated through. Stir in cilantro. Serve with sour cream.   *Makes 4 servings*

■ Gilroy Garlic Soup ■

3 tablespoons olive oil
1 large sweet onion, chopped
1 leek, white part only, washed well and diced
8 cups chicken broth
2 large potatoes, peeled and cubed
15 cloves CHRISTOPHER RANCH Whole Peeled Garlic
1 cup half-and-half
Salt and black pepper
½ cup snipped chives

Heat oil in Dutch oven over medium heat. Add onion and leek; cook and stir until tender. Add broth; bring to a boil. Add potatoes and garlic; simmer for 1 hour. Place potato mixture and half-and-half in food processor; process until smooth. Season to taste with salt and pepper. Top with chives.
Makes 6 to 8 servings

Chili Verde

Chili-Crusted Grilled Chicken Caesar ■ Salad ■

¼ cup lemon juice, divided
4 teaspoons minced garlic, divided
2 teaspoons grated lemon peel
1½ teaspoons dried oregano leaves, divided
1 teaspoon chili powder
1 pound boneless skinless chicken breasts
1 tablespoon olive oil
2 anchovy fillets, minced
1 large head romaine lettuce, cut into 1-inch strips
¼ cup grated Parmesan cheese
Tortilla chips (optional)

1. Combine 1 tablespoon juice, 3 teaspoons garlic, lemon peel, 1 teaspoon oregano and chili powder in small bowl. Rub chicken completely with chili mixture.

2. To prevent sticking, spray grid with nonstick cooking spray. Prepare coals for grilling. Grill chicken 4 to 6 inches above medium-high coals for 5 to 7 minutes or until marks are established and surface is dry. Turn chicken over; grill 3 to 4 minutes or until chicken is no longer pink in center.

3. Combine remaining 3 tablespoons lemon juice, remaining 1 teaspoon garlic, remaining ½ teaspoon oregano, oil and anchovy in large bowl. Add lettuce to bowl; toss to coat with dressing. Sprinkle with cheese; toss.

4. Arrange salad on 4 large plates. Slice chicken. Fan on each salad. Garnish with tortilla chips, if desired. *Makes 4 servings*

Chili-Crusted Grilled Chicken Caesar Salad

VEGETABLES & SIDES

Rosemary-Garlic
■ Mashed Potatoes ■

2½ pounds Yukon Gold
    potatoes (5 medium),
    peeled and cut into 1-inch
    pieces
1½ teaspoons salt, divided
 ½ cup heavy cream
 ½ cup milk
  2 tablespoons butter
  1 tablespoon minced fresh
    rosemary *or* 1 teaspoon
    dried rosemary
  1 large head roasted garlic
    (page 279)
 ⅛ teaspoon white pepper

Place potato pieces in medium
saucepan; add water to cover and
1 teaspoon salt. Bring to a boil over
high heat. Reduce heat to medium-
low; simmer, uncovered, about
12 to 15 minutes until pieces are
tender when pierced with fork. (Do
not overcook.) Drain water from
pan; cover and set aside.

Place cream, milk, butter and
rosemary in small saucepan; heat
over medium-high heat about
3 minutes or until butter melts and
mixture simmers, stirring often.
Mash potatoes with potato masher
until smooth. Add roasted garlic
and milk mixture; beat with electric
mixer until smooth. Beat in
remaining ½ teaspoon salt and
pepper. Serve hot.

Makes 4 to 6 servings

Rosemary-Garlic Mashed Potatoes

Lemon-Garlic Broccoli over Spaghetti ■ Squash ■

   1 spaghetti squash (2 pounds)
   1 can (about 14 ounces)
      chicken broth
  10 large cloves garlic, halved
   2 tablespoons lemon juice
   3 fresh sage leaves
   2 cups broccoli florets

1. Place spaghetti squash in large saucepan. Pierce skin with fork. Add enough water to cover. Bring to a boil over high heat. Reduce heat to low; simmer, covered, 20 to 30 minutes or until squash is soft. Cut squash in half lengthwise; remove seeds. Set aside.

2. Meanwhile, combine broth and garlic in small saucepan. Bring to a boil over high heat. Reduce heat to low; simmer 15 minutes or until tender. Remove from heat; cool slightly.

3. Place broth, garlic, juice and sage in food processor; process until smooth. Return mixture to saucepan; keep warm.

4. Combine broccoli and ¼ cup water in large nonstick skillet with tight-fitting lid. Bring to a boil over high heat. Reduce heat to medium. Cover and steam 5 minutes or until broccoli is crisp-tender.

5. Scoop out inside of squash. Place squash and broccoli in medium bowl; pour lemon-garlic mixture over squash mixture. Mix well. Garnish as desired. Serve immediately.   *Makes 6 servings*

■ Garlic Stir-Fry ■

   ¼ cup vegetable oil
   4 cloves CHRISTOPHER
      RANCH Whole Peeled
      Garlic, crushed
   3 small slices fresh ginger
      Fresh vegetables cut into
         bite-size pieces, such as
         zucchini, broccoli, onions,
         bell peppers, carrots
   ½ cup white wine
   1 teaspoon salt
   ½ teaspoon black pepper
      Chopped fresh oregano
      Chopped fresh parsley
      Juice of ½ lemon

Heat oil in large skillet over medium-high heat. Add garlic and ginger; cook and stir until ginger is golden brown. Discard ginger. Add vegetables; stir to coat. Add wine; cook and stir 3 minutes. Add salt, pepper, oregano, parsley and lemon juice to taste. Cook 1 minute more.
Makes 4 to 6 servings

Lemon-Garlic Broccoli over Spaghetti Squash

Stuffed Jumbo Shells with ■ Garlic Vegetables ■

Garlic Vegetables (recipe follows)
2 cups ricotta cheese
1 package (10 ounces) frozen chopped spinach, thawed and squeezed dry
¼ cup grated Parmesan cheese
2 cloves garlic, minced
¾ teaspoon dried marjoram leaves
½ to 1 teaspoon salt
½ teaspoon dried basil leaves
½ teaspoon black pepper
¼ teaspoon dried thyme leaves
12 jumbo pasta shells, cooked according to package directions, drained and cooled
Grated Parmesan cheese

Prepare Garlic Vegetables. Spoon into 10-inch round baking dish.

Combine ricotta, spinach, ¼ cup grated Parmesan cheese, garlic, marjoram, salt, basil, pepper and thyme in medium bowl. Spoon cheese mixture into shells.

Preheat oven to 350°F. Arrange shells on top of Garlic Vegetables. Carefully spoon sauce from vegetables over shells. Bake, loosely covered with foil, 35 to 40 minutes or until stuffed shells are heated through. Sprinkle Parmesan cheese over shells. *Makes 4 servings*

Garlic Vegetables

2 tablespoons olive oil, divided
1 large head garlic, coarsely chopped
⅓ cup sun-dried tomatoes (not packed in oil)
2 tablespoons all-purpose flour
1¼ cups canned vegetable broth
2 large carrots, sliced diagonally
1 medium zucchini, halved and sliced
1 medium yellow summer squash, halved and sliced
2 tablespoons minced fresh parsley
Salt and black pepper

Stuffed Jumbo Shells with Garlic Vegetables

Heat 1 tablespoon oil in small skillet over medium heat. Add garlic; cook and stir 2 to 3 minutes. Reduce heat to low and cook about 15 minutes or until garlic is golden brown, stirring frequently. Add tomatoes; cook over medium heat 2 minutes. Stir in flour. Cook and stir 2 minutes. Gradually stir in vegetable broth. Cook 1 to 2 minutes or until sauce thickens, stirring constantly.

Heat remaining 1 tablespoon oil in medium skillet over medium heat. Add carrots; cook and stir 2 minutes. Add zucchini and squash; cook and stir 3 minutes or until crisp-tender. Remove from heat. Stir garlic mixture and parsley into carrot mixture in skillet. Season to taste with salt and pepper. *Makes 2 cups*

Summer Garden
■ Harvest Fusilli ■

¼ cup olive oil
8 ounces mushrooms,
    trimmed and sliced
1 red bell pepper, diced
1 green bell pepper, diced
1 yellow bell pepper, diced
3 shallots, chopped
10 green onions, chopped
1 large onion, chopped
8 cloves garlic, crushed
¼ teaspoon red pepper flakes
4 cups chopped seeded
    tomatoes
½ cup chopped fresh basil
2 tablespoons chopped fresh
    oregano
    Salt and black pepper
1 package (16 ounces) fusilli,
    cooked according to
    package directions,
    drained

Heat oil in large skillet over medium-high heat. Cook and stir mushrooms, bell peppers, shallots, onions, garlic and red pepper flakes until lightly browned. Add tomatoes with juice; bring to a boil. Reduce heat to low; simmer, uncovered, 20 minutes. Stir in basil and oregano. Season to taste with salt and black pepper.

Place fusilli on plates. Spoon sauce over fusilli. Garnish, if desired.

Makes 6 to 8 servings

Thailand Peanut
■ Pesto ■

1 cup unsalted roasted
    peanuts
½ cup soy sauce
½ cup sesame oil
1 teaspoon TABASCO® brand
    Pepper Sauce
¼ cup honey
⅓ cup water
3 cloves garlic, minced
12 ounces bow tie pasta,
    cooked according to
    package directions,
    drained
    Chopped scallions for
    garnish

Place peanuts in food processor; process until finely ground. With motor running, add soy sauce, sesame oil, TABASCO® Sauce, honey, water and garlic, one at a time, through the feed tube. Process until a thick, smooth paste has formed. Transfer the mixture to a bowl; refrigerate, covered, until ready to use. Toss with bow tie pasta and garnish with chopped scallions.

Makes 4 servings

Summer Garden Harvest Fusilli

French Pan-Roasted ■ Hens ■

1 package (about 3 pounds) PERDUE® Fresh Split Cornish Hens
3 tablespoons olive oil, divided
1 tablespoon herbes de Provence
Salt and black pepper
3 garlic cloves, peeled, divided
½ cup white wine or water

Rub hens with 1 tablespoon oil; sprinkle with herbes de Provence, and salt and pepper to taste. Heat remaining 2 tablespoons oil in large, deep skillet over medium-high heat. Add hens and 2 garlic cloves. Brown hens lightly on both sides. Discard cooked garlic and add remaining garlic clove. Reduce heat to low; cover and cook 30 to 40 minutes until hens are browned and cooked through, turning 2 to 3 times.

Remove to warm serving platter; discard garlic. Add wine to skillet; cook 1 minute, stirring to incorporate pan juices. Serve hens with pan sauce.

Makes 2 to 4 servings

■ Turkey Jambalaya ■

1 tablespoon vegetable oil, divided
6 ounces turkey ham, cut into ½-inch cubes
6 ounces fully cooked smoked turkey sausage or kielbasa, cut into ¼-inch slices
1½ cups chopped onions
1½ cups ¼-inch celery slices
1 cup ½-inch green bell pepper cubes
4 to 5 cloves garlic, minced
2 tablespoons Creole seasoning
1¼ cups uncooked long-grain rice
2 cups turkey or chicken broth
1 can (15 ounces) tomato sauce

1. Heat 1 teaspoon oil in large saucepan over medium heat. Add turkey ham and sausage; cook and stir until lightly browned on all sides. Remove from pan; set aside.

2. Heat remaining oil in same saucepan. Add onions, celery, bell pepper, garlic and Creole seasoning; cook and stir about 10 minutes or until vegetables are crisp-tender.

3. Add rice; cook an additional 5 minutes, stirring constantly to prevent sticking. Add turkey broth, tomato sauce and reserved turkey ham and sausage; bring to a boil. Reduce heat; cover and simmer 25 to 30 minutes or until rice is tender. *Makes 4 servings*

Favorite recipe from **National Turkey Federation**

Roasted Chicken and ■ Veggies ■

1 chicken (3 to 5 pounds), washed and patted dry
6 CHRISTOPHER RANCH Pearl Onions, peeled
6 cloves CHRISTOPHER RANCH Elephant Garlic, peeled
6 CHRISTOPHER RANCH Shallots, peeled
6 small carrots, peeled and cut in half crosswise
3 potatoes, scrubbed and cut in ½-inch slices
¼ cup olive oil
½ cup white wine
  Italian seasoning
  Seasoned salt
  Lemon pepper
4 fresh rosemary sprigs

Place chicken in large baking dish. Toss onions, garlic, shallots, carrots and potatoes with olive oil in large bowl to coat; place around chicken. Pour wine over vegetables and chicken; season to taste with Italian seasoning, seasoned salt and lemon pepper. Place rosemary sprigs over chicken and vegetables. Bake at 450°F for 1 to 1½ hours, basting frequently. Remove rosemary sprigs before serving. *Makes 4 servings*

Note: Onions, garlic and shallots have a milder flavor when baked, so serve them along with the other baked vegetables.

Turkey Breast Braised
■ with Garlic and Rice ■

- 1 cup uncooked long-grain rice
- 1 can (about 14 ounces) chicken broth
- ½ cup white wine
- 2 teaspoons dried parsley flakes
- ½ teaspoon dried rosemary
- ½ teaspoon dried thyme leaves
- ½ teaspoon dried sage leaves
- 1 bay leaf
- 1 bone-in turkey breast (6 pounds)
- Paprika
- 3 heads of garlic, root-end cut off

1. Combine rice, chicken broth, wine, parsley, rosemary, thyme, sage and bay leaf in ovenproof Dutch oven. Place turkey over rice mixture and sprinkle turkey generously with paprika. Place whole garlic heads, cut end up, in rice around turkey breast. Cover top of ovenproof Dutch oven with foil and lid. Bake at 350°F 2½ to 3 hours or until meat thermometer inserted in thickest part of breast registers 170° to 175°F. Allow to stand 10 to 15 minutes. Remove bay leaf; discard.

Turkey Breast Braised with Garlic and Rice

2. To serve, carve turkey into slices and place on platter. Spoon rice mixture into serving bowl. Squeeze garlic from skins onto turkey and rice. *Makes 4 servings*

Favorite recipe from **National Turkey Federation**

■ Ginger Hot Thighs ■

2 tablespoons olive oil
1 package (about 1¾ pounds) PERDUE® Fresh Skinless Chicken Thighs
1 onion, finely chopped
¼ cup red wine
4 garlic cloves, minced
1 tablespoon grated fresh ginger
1½ teaspoons ground cumin
½ teaspoon chili powder
1 tablespoon minced fresh parsley

Heat oil in large nonstick skillet over medium heat. Add chicken; cook 7 to 8 minutes on each side or until browned. Combine onion, wine, garlic, ginger, cumin and chili powder in small bowl. Add to skillet; partially cover and reduce heat to medium-low. Cook about 20 to 30 minutes or until chicken is fork-tender and liquid has been reduced to a glaze. Sprinkle with parsley and serve.

Makes 3 to 4 servings

■ Forty Clove Chicken ■

3 pounds chicken pieces
40 cloves CHRISTOPHER RANCH Whole Peeled Garlic (unpeeled cloves may also be used)
½ cup dry white wine
¼ cup dry vermouth
¼ cup olive oil
4 ribs celery, cut into 1-inch pieces
2 teaspoons dry basil leaves, crushed
1 teaspoon dry oregano leaves, crushed
6 sprigs fresh parsley, minced
Pinch of red pepper flakes
Salt and black pepper
1 lemon, cut in half

Preheat oven to 375°F. Place chicken in shallow baking pan, skin side up. Sprinkle chicken evenly with garlic, wine, vermouth, oil, celery, basil, oregano, parsley, red pepper, and salt and black pepper to taste. Squeeze juice from lemon over top. Cut lemon peel into pieces and arrange throughout chicken. Cover with foil and bake for 40 minutes. Remove foil and bake an additional 15 minutes. Serve garlic cloves with chicken or spread on sliced French bread. (If left unpeeled, just squeeze out pulp.) *Makes 4 servings*

Baked Chicken with Crispy Cheese-Garlic ■ Crust ■

1 teaspoon olive oil
½ cup chopped garlic (one large head)
4 tablespoons water, divided
½ cup dry bread crumbs
¼ cup Dijon mustard (or more to taste)
1 cup (4 ounces) shredded JARLSBERG Cheese
3 pounds chicken pieces, skin removed and trimmed of fat

Preheat oven to 400°F. Heat oil in large skillet over high heat. Add garlic; cook and stir 2 minutes. Add 2 tablespoons water; cover tightly. Reduce heat to low; cook 4 minutes.

Meanwhile, mix crumbs and mustard. Add garlic and blend well. Add cheese plus remaining 2 tablespoons water and mix to make a paste.

Arrange chicken on rack in foil-lined baking pan. Pat thin layer of garlic-cheese paste on top side of chicken pieces to form a crust. Bake, loosely tented with foil, 1 hour or until juices run clear when pierced with a knife.

Makes 3 to 4 servings

Garlic Chicken and ■ Corn Stir-Fry ■

4 boneless skinless chicken thighs, cut into 1-inch squares
1 tablespoon soy sauce
4 cloves garlic, minced
¼ teaspoon black pepper
½ cup chicken broth
¾ teaspoon onion powder
1½ teaspoons cornstarch
2 teaspoons vegetable oil
1 large red bell pepper, cut into 1-inch squares
2 large ribs celery, cut into 1-inch slices
1 package (10 ounces) frozen corn, thawed and drained
2 cups hot cooked rice

Place chicken in small bowl. Add soy sauce, garlic and black pepper; stir to coat. Marinate 15 minutes at room temperature.

Meanwhile, stir chicken broth and onion powder into cornstarch in small bowl until smooth; set aside. Heat oil in wok over high heat. Reduce heat to medium-high. Add chicken; stir-fry 2 minutes. Add bell pepper and celery; stir-fry 2 minutes. Add corn; cook and stir 3 minutes. Stir in cornstarch mixture; cook and stir over high heat until mixture boils and slightly thickens. Serve over rice.

Makes 4 servings

Jen's Ginger-Garlic ■ Chicken Drummettes ■

½ cup soy sauce
¼ cup white wine
2 teaspoons sugar
2 teaspoons CHRISTOPHER
    RANCH Chopped Ginger
    or 1 teaspoon fresh grated
    ginger
Juice of 2 to 3 lemons
3 cloves CHRISTOPHER
    RANCH Whole Peeled
    Garlic, crushed
14 chicken drummettes

To prepare marinade, combine soy sauce, wine, sugar, ginger, lemon juice and garlic in small bowl. Place drummettes in resealable plastic food storage bag. Pour marinade over drummettes. Press air out of bag and seal tightly. Turn bag over to completely coat drummettes with marinade. Refrigerate 6 hours or overnight, turning bag once or twice. Place drummettes with marinade in a large glass baking dish sprayed with nonstick cooking spray. Bake at 350°F for 1 hour or until juices run clear. Marinade should form a glaze on drummettes.   *Makes 4 servings*

Garlicky Chicken ■ Packets ■

1 cup julienned carrots
½ cup sliced onion
¼ cup chopped fresh basil *or*
    1 tablespoon dried basil
    leaves, crushed
2 tablespoons mayonnaise
6 cloves garlic, minced
⅛ teaspoon black pepper
4 boneless skinless chicken
    breast halves

Cut parchment paper or foil into four 12-inch squares. Fold squares in half, then cut into shape of half hearts. Open parchment to form whole hearts.

Preheat oven to 400°F. Place carrots and onion on 1 side of each heart near fold. Combine basil, mayonnaise, garlic and pepper in small bowl; spread mixture on chicken. Place chicken, mayonnaise side up, on top of vegetables. Fold parchment over chicken; seal by creasing and folding edges of parchment in small overlapping sections from top of heart until completed at point. Finish by twisting point and tucking under.

Place parchment packages on ungreased baking sheet. Bake 20 to 25 minutes or until juices run clear and chicken is no longer pink in center.   *Makes 4 servings*

Lamb Brochettes with ■ Plums ■

2 tablespoons minced fresh
  cilantro
2 tablespoons olive oil
1 tablespoon lemon juice
3 teaspoons cumin, divided
5 medium garlic cloves,
  minced
1½ teaspoons salt, divided
1 teaspoon curry powder
¼ teaspoon ground red pepper
¼ teaspoon black pepper
1½ pounds leg of lamb,
  trimmed, cut into 1-inch
  cubes
8 fresh California plums, cut
  into wedges

To prepare marinade, combine
cilantro, olive oil, lemon juice,
2 teaspoons cumin, garlic,
1 teaspoon salt, curry powder, red
pepper and black pepper in large
nonreactive bowl. Add lamb and
toss well. Cover with plastic wrap;
marinate lamb in refrigerator for
2 hours or overnight. Drain lamb;
reserve marinade.

Starting with lamb, alternately
thread 4 lamb cubes and 4 plum
wedges onto metal skewers.* Brush
with reserved marinade; sprinkle
with remaining 1 teaspoon cumin
and remaining ½ teaspoon salt.

Prepare coals for grilling or preheat
broiler and cook, turning skewers
occasionally, until lamb is medium-
rare, 8 to 10 minutes. Transfer the
brochettes to a serving platter or
individual plates.

Makes 6 servings
(2 kabobs each)

*If using bamboo skewers, soak in cold water
10 to 15 minutes to prevent burning.*

Favorite Recipe from **California Tree Fruit
Agreement**

Pork Chops in ■ Creamy Garlic Sauce ■

1 cup chicken broth
¼ cup garlic cloves, peeled
  and crushed (about
  12 to 15)
½ teaspoon olive oil
4 boneless pork loin chops,
  about ¼ inch thick each
1 tablespoon minced fresh
  parsley
½ teaspoon dried tarragon
  leaves
¼ teaspoon salt
¼ teaspoon black pepper
1 tablespoon all-purpose flour
2 tablespoons water
1 tablespoon dry sherry
2 cups cooked white rice

1. Place chicken broth and garlic in small saucepan. Bring to a boil over high heat. Cover; reduce heat to low. Simmer 25 to 30 minutes or until garlic mashes easily with fork. Set aside to cool. Process in blender or food processor until smooth.

2. Heat olive oil in large nonstick skillet over medium-high heat. Add pork; cook 1 to 1½ minutes on each side or until browned. Pour garlic mixture into skillet. Sprinkle with parsley, tarragon, salt and pepper. Bring to a boil; cover. Reduce heat to low; simmer 10 to 15 minutes or until pork is juicy and barely pink in center. Remove pork from skillet; keep warm.

3. Combine flour and water in small cup. Slowly pour flour mixture into skillet; bring to a boil. Cook and stir until mixture thickens. Stir in sherry. Serve sauce over pork and rice. Garnish as desired.   *Makes 4 servings*

Pork Chops in Creamy Garlic Sauce

■ Fajitas ■

½ cup lime juice *or* ¼ cup
    lime juice and ¼ cup
    tequila or beer
1 tablespoon minced garlic
1 tablespoon dried oregano
    leaves
2 teaspoons ground cumin
2 teaspoons black pepper
1 pound flank steak
6 (10-inch) flour tortillas or
    12 (7-inch) flour tortillas
4 bell peppers, any color,
    halved
1 large bunch green onions
    Salsa Cruda (page 167)
1 cup coarsely chopped fresh
    cilantro
1 ripe avocado, thinly sliced
6 tablespoons sour cream

1. To prepare marinade, combine lime juice, garlic, oregano, cumin and black pepper in small bowl. Place flank steak in resealable plastic food storage bag; pour marinade over steak. Press air from bag and seal; turn bag to coat. Refrigerate 30 minutes or up to 24 hours.

2. Place tortillas in stacks of 3. Wrap each stack in foil; set aside.

3. Drain marinade from meat into small saucepan. Bring to a boil over high heat. Remove from heat; set aside.

4. To prevent sticking, spray grid with nonstick cooking spray. Adjust grid 4 to 6 inches above heat. Prepare coals for grilling. Place meat in center of grill over medium-hot coals. Place bell peppers, skin side down, around meat; cover. Grill peppers 6 minutes or until skin is spotted with brown. Turn over and continue grilling 6 to 8 minutes or until tender. Move to sides of grill to keep warm while meat finishes grilling.

5. Grill meat, basting frequently with marinade, 8 minutes or until brown. Turn; grill 8 to 10 minutes or until slightly pink in center for medium doneness. During the last 4 minutes of grilling, brush onions with remaining marinade; grill 1 to 2 minutes. Turn; grill 1 to 2 minutes more or until tender.

6. Place wrapped packets of tortillas on grill; heat about 5 minutes. Slice peppers and onions into thin 2-inch-long strips. Thinly slice meat across the grain.

7. Place tortilla on plate. Place meat, peppers, onions, Salsa Cruda and cilantro in center of each tortilla. Fold sides completely over filling to enclose. Serve with avocado and sour cream.

Makes 6 servings

Fajitas

Provençal-Style Lamb
■ Shanks ■

2 tablespoons olive oil
4 lamb shanks (about
    1 pound each)
2 large onions, chopped
5 cloves garlic, minced,
    divided
1 can (28 ounces) Italian-style
    plum tomatoes, undrained
    and coarsely chopped
½ cup dry vermouth
1½ teaspoons dried basil leaves
1½ teaspoons dried rosemary
1 teaspoon salt
½ teaspoon black pepper
1 can (19 ounces) cannellini
    beans, rinsed and drained
1½ tablespoons balsamic
    vinegar (optional)
2 tablespoons chopped fresh
    Italian parsley
1 teaspoon grated lemon peel

Heat 1 tablespoon oil in Dutch oven over medium heat; add 2 lamb shanks. Brown on all sides; transfer to large plate with tongs. Repeat with remaining 1 tablespoon oil and 2 lamb shanks.

Add onions and 4 cloves garlic to drippings in Dutch oven; cook 6 to 8 minutes until onions are tender, stirring occasionally. Add tomatoes with liquid, vermouth, basil, rosemary, salt and pepper; bring to a boil over medium-high heat. Return shanks to Dutch oven. Reduce heat to low; cover and simmer 1½ hours or until shanks are tender.

Remove shanks; cool slightly. Skim fat from pan juices with large spoon; discard. Stir beans into pan juices; heat through. Cut lamb from shanks into 1-inch pieces; discard bones and gristle. Return lamb to Dutch oven; heat through. Stir in vinegar.

Combine parsley, lemon peel and remaining clove garlic in small bowl. To serve, ladle lamb mixture into 6 individual shallow serving bowls; sprinkle with parsley mixture. Garnish, if desired.

Makes 6 servings

Provençal-Style Lamb Shanks

Tuscan-Style Lamb
■ with White Beans ■

 1 pound large dried lima
    (butter) beans
 1 teaspoon olive oil
 3 pounds lamb shoulder, cut
    into large pieces (fat
    trimmed)
 3 onions, peeled and
    quartered
 2 carrots, peeled and
    quartered
12 large cloves garlic, sliced
 1 cup dry vermouth or red or
    white wine* (optional)
 3 cups chicken broth
 1 cup chopped celery, with
    leaves
 2 bay leaves
 2 large sprigs rosemary *or*
    1 tablespoon dried
    rosemary, crumbled
 1 to 2 cups (4 to 8 ounces)
    shredded JARLSBERG
    Cheese

*Note: If not using vermouth or wine, increase
chicken broth to 4 cups.*

Rinse beans; place in large saucepan. Cover with 2 inches water. Bring to a boil over high heat; boil 2 minutes. Remove from heat; cover and let soak 1 hour. Drain beans; discard water. (Or soak beans in cold water overnight, drain and discard water.)

Heat oil in Dutch oven over high heat. Add lamb; cook and stir 10 minutes. Add onions, carrots and garlic; cook and stir 8 minutes, lifting lamb off bottom of pan to let vegetables cook.

Add vermouth, if desired, and cook 3 minutes. Add broth, celery, bay leaves and rosemary; cover and simmer 1½ hours. Add beans and shredded Jarlsberg and continue to simmer 40 minutes to 1 hour until beans are desired firmness. Remove bay leaves and discard before serving.   *Makes 8 servings*

My Favorite Recipes

Favorite recipe: _____

Favorite recipe from: _____

Ingredients: _____

_____

_____

_____

_____

_____

Method: _____

_____

_____

_____

_____

_____

_____

_____

_____

_____

_____

_____

My Favorite Recipes

Favorite recipe: _____

Favorite recipe from: _____

Ingredients: _____
_____
_____
_____
_____
_____

Method: _____
_____
_____
_____
_____
_____
_____
_____
_____
_____
_____

My Favorite Recipes

Favorite recipe: _____

Favorite recipe from: _____

Ingredients: _____

_____

_____

_____

_____

_____

Method: _____

_____

_____

_____

_____

_____

_____

_____

_____

_____

_____

_____

Favorite recipe: _____

Favorite recipe from: _____

Ingredients: _____

_____

_____

_____

_____

_____

Method: _____

_____

_____

_____

_____

_____

_____

_____

_____

_____

_____

_____

My Favorite Recipes

Favorite recipe: _____

Favorite recipe from: _____

Ingredients: _____

_____

_____

_____

_____

_____

Method: _____

_____

_____

_____

_____

_____

_____

_____

_____

_____

_____

My Favorite Recipes

Favorite recipe: _____

Favorite recipe from: _____

Ingredients: _____

_____

_____

_____

_____

_____

Method: _____

_____

_____

_____

_____

_____

_____

_____

_____

_____

_____

My Favorite Recipes

Favorite recipe: _____

Favorite recipe from: _____

Ingredients: _____

_____

_____

_____

_____

_____

Method: _____

_____

_____

_____

_____

_____

_____

_____

_____

_____

_____

_____

My Favorite Recipes

Favorite recipe: _____

Favorite recipe from: _____

Ingredients: _____

_____

_____

_____

_____

_____

Method: _____

_____

_____

_____

_____

_____

_____

_____

_____

_____

_____

My Favorite Recipes

Favorite recipe: _____

Favorite recipe from: _____

Ingredients: _____

_____

_____

_____

_____

_____

Method: _____

_____

_____

_____

_____

_____

_____

_____

_____

_____

_____

My Favorite Recipes

Favorite recipe: _____

Favorite recipe from: _____

Ingredients: _____

_____

_____

_____

_____

_____

Method: _____

_____

_____

_____

_____

_____

_____

_____

_____

_____

My Favorite Recipes

Favorite recipe: _____

Favorite recipe from: _____

Ingredients: _____

_____

_____

_____

_____

_____

Method: _____

_____

_____

_____

_____

_____

_____

_____

_____

_____

_____

_____

My Favorite Recipes

Favorite recipe: _____

Favorite recipe from: _____

Ingredients: _____

_____

_____

_____

_____

Method: _____

_____

_____

_____

_____

_____

_____

_____

_____

_____

Favorite recipe: _____

Favorite recipe from: _____

Ingredients: _____

_____

_____

_____

_____

_____

Method: _____

_____

_____

_____

_____

_____

_____

_____

_____

_____

_____

My Favorite Recipes

Favorite recipe: _____

Favorite recipe from: _____

Ingredients: _____

_____

_____

_____

_____

_____

Method: _____

_____

_____

_____

_____

_____

_____

_____

_____

_____

_____

_____

My Favorite Recipes

Favorite recipe: _____

Favorite recipe from: _____

Ingredients: _____

_____

_____

_____

_____

_____

Method: _____

_____

_____

_____

_____

_____

_____

_____

_____

_____

_____

_____

My Favorite Recipes

Favorite recipe: _____

Favorite recipe from: _____

Ingredients: _____

_____

_____

_____

_____

Method: _____

_____

_____

_____

_____

_____

_____

_____

_____

_____

_____

My Favorite Recipes

Favorite recipe: _____

Favorite recipe from: _____

Ingredients: _____
_____
_____
_____
_____
_____

Method: _____
_____
_____
_____
_____
_____
_____
_____
_____
_____

My Favorite Recipes

Favorite recipe: _____

Favorite recipe from: _____

Ingredients: _____

_____

_____

_____

_____

_____

Method: _____

_____

_____

_____

_____

_____

_____

_____

_____

_____

_____

_____

My Favorite Recipes

Favorite recipe: _____

Favorite recipe from: _____

Ingredients: _____

_____

_____

_____

_____

_____

Method: _____

_____

_____

_____

_____

_____

_____

_____

_____

_____

_____

My Favorite Recipes

Favorite recipe: _____

Favorite recipe from: _____

Ingredients: _____
_____
_____
_____
_____
_____

Method: _____
_____
_____
_____
_____
_____
_____
_____
_____
_____
_____
_____

My Favorite Dinner Party

Date: _____

Occasion: _____
_____

Guests: _____
_____
_____
_____
_____

Menu: _____
_____
_____
_____
_____
_____
_____
_____
_____
_____
_____
_____

My Favorite Brunch

Date: _____

Occasion: _____

_____

Guests: _____

_____

_____

_____

_____

Menu: _____

_____

_____

_____

_____

_____

_____

_____

_____

_____

_____

_____

_____

_____

My Favorite Brunch

Date: _____

Occasion: _____

_____

Guests: _____

_____

_____

_____

_____

Menu: _____

_____

_____

_____

_____

_____

_____

_____

_____

_____

_____

_____

_____

My Favorite Brunch

Date: _____

Occasion: _____

_____

Guests: _____

_____

_____

_____

_____

Menu: _____

_____

_____

_____

_____

_____

_____

_____

_____

_____

_____

_____

My Favorite Food Gifts

Friend: _____

Date: _____

Food Gift: _____

_____

_____

_____

_____

_____

_____

_____

_____

_____

_____

_____

_____

_____

_____

_____

_____

_____

_____

_____

_____

_____

My Favorite Food Gifts

Friend: _____

Date: _____

Food Gift: _____

_____

_____

_____

_____

_____

_____

_____

_____

_____

_____

_____

_____

_____

_____

_____

_____

_____

My Favorite Friends

Friend: _____

Favorite foods: _____

_____

_____

_____

_____

_____

Don't serve: _____

_____

_____

_____

_____

_____

_____

_____

_____

_____

_____

_____

_____

My Favorite Friends

Friend: _____

Favorite foods: _____

_____

_____

_____

_____

Don't serve: _____

_____

_____

_____

_____

_____

_____

_____

_____

_____

Potato Tips

Cultivated as early as 3000 B.C. and grown in over a hundred varieties, the potato is easily the most popular vegetable in the United States. In fact, it is estimated that potatoes are included in one-third of all meals that Americans eat. And we enjoy them in almost as many preparations as there are varieties of potatoes.

The potato may have its roots in ancient Peru but today it is grown in more than 80 countries. Originally thought to be poisonous, this undergrown tuber became a staple food in Ireland until failure of the crop led to widespread famine and massive emigration in the 1940's. Potatoes, when prepared with little additional fat, are low in calories and sodium and are a good source of vitamins, minerals and fiber.

Different potatoes are better for different preparations:

• Russets are popular for baking, mashing and for French fries. They are large (up to 18 ounces each) and oval in shape with rough brown skin and starchy flesh. Russet Burbank, also referred to as Idaho or russet, is the leading variety.

• Long whites are an all-purpose potato with thin pale brown skin They average about eight ounces each. They can be baked, boiled or fried.

• Round whites are good for boiling and mashing. Smaller than long whites with a light tan skin, they are similar to round red potatoes.

• Round reds have a smooth red skin, and because of their lower starch and higher moisture content, they are good for boiling and mashing.

A number of specialty varieties are becoming available in some supermarkets and farmers' markets. Yukon gold potatoes, with a skin and flesh that ranges from yellow to buttery gold, have a rich moist texture that is ideal for mashing. Blue potatoes have a delicate flavor with blue to purple skin and flesh.

New potatoes are freshly dug young potatoes. They may be any variety, but most often are round reds. New potatoes can be as small as marbles or almost as large as full-size potatoes, but they should have a very thin wispy skin. The sugar in these young potatoes has not completely converted to starch so they have a crisp, waxy texture.

Buying Tips: Select potatoes based on their intended use. Choose potatoes that are clean, firm, smooth, well-shaped and free from sprouts. Any "eyes" should be minimal and shallow. Skins should be dry and without wrinkles and cracks. Avoid potatoes with black spots or green-tinged skins, which are an indication that they were stored incorrectly and exposed to sunlight—these potatoes could be bitter as well as toxic if eaten in quantity.

Storage: Store potatoes in a cool, dry dark location (light and warmth encourage sprouting) for up to two weeks. They may be stored in a paper or burlap bag (not plastic). Check them occasionally and remove any potatoes that have sprouted or begun to shrivel. One rotten potato can spoil the whole lot. Avoid storing potatoes and onions together as the gases given off by the onions can cause the potatoes to spoil more quickly. Avoid storing potatoes in the refrigerator as the starch turns to sugar, making them overly sweet. New potatoes, if not used within a few days, should be refrigerated.

Basic Preparation: Before cooking, scrub potatoes with a vegetable brush to remove embedded dirt. For many uses, potatoes do not need to be peeled. When peeling, use a swivel-bladed vegetable peeler rather than a knife. The skin and the flesh below the skin are rich in vitamins, so peel away as little of the flesh as possible. Cut out the "eyes" and any blemishes, and trim away any green skin or flesh. Peeled potatoes should be immediately covered with water, as the surface discolors quickly. Sliced or cut-up potatoes speed up cooking; pieces of similar thickness ensure even cooking. Before baking or microwaving potatoes, pierce the skin with a fork to allow steam to escape and prevent them from exploding.

Onions have been used since prehistoric times. They continue to play an essential role in cuisines around the world. Like asparagus and garlic, onions are a member of the lily family. They are used both as a seasoning and a vegetable.

Varieties: There are two types of onions, green and dry.

• Green onions, or scallions, are onions that are harvested when immature. They are long and finger-thin with white bases and green tops, both of which are edible. They are sold in bunches. Green onions are easy to grow in a home garden. If you plant them every few weeks, you will have a constant supply during the entire growing season.

All other onions are classified as dry onions, meaning that they are harvested when mature and then allowed to dry until their skins are papery. This group includes Bermuda, globe, pearl, red, Spanish, Vidalia, Maui and Walla Walla.

• Bermuda onions are mild-flavored onions with an oval shape and white skin that has subtle vertical green stripes. They are sweet during the peak of the season (early fall) when they are good raw, but become stronger when stored.

• Globe onions (also called yellow onions) are the most common of the dry onions. They are round and small or medium in size with yellowish-gold skins and a strong flavor. Use them for cooking. Globe onions are generally more economical; and they keep for some time.

• Pearl onions are tiny white onions with a mild flavor. They are usually cooked whole; they make good additions to stews. Pearl onions are also pickled.

• Red onions (also called Italian onions) may be round, oval or slightly flat. They are covered with a dark red to purple skin. When cut, their rings of whitish flesh are outlined in purple. Red onions are generally sweet unless they have been stored for a long time.

• Spanish onions are large and round with a caramel-colored skin. These are fairly sweet and can be eaten raw.

• Vidalia, Maui and Walla Walla are all very sweet onions. They have taken their names from the areas where they grow: Vidalia, Georgia; Maui, Hawaii, and Walla Walla, Washington. Vidalia are generally the sweetest.

Availability: Green onions are available all year. They are most abundant in the spring and summer. Bermuda, Spanish and red onions are available all year but they are sweeter in the late summer and early fall. Sweet onion varieties have short seasons: Maui from April to July, Vidalia from May to June, Walla Walla from June to September.

Buying Tips: Green onions should have firm white bottoms and crisp green tops. Dry onions should feel heavy for their size, dry and firm to the touch with no soft spots or sprouts. Onions should smell mild when purchased. Avoid those with excess dirt or dark spots as this may indicate that mold is present.

Yield: 1 pound onions = 3 large or 4 medium onions; 2 to 3 cups chopped.
1 green onion = 1 or 2 tablespoons sliced or chopped.

Storage: Store green onions in the refrigerator in a plastic bag for up to five days. All other onions should be stored in a cool, dry area with good air circulation for up to two months. Sweet onions may not store for quite as long. Check them periodically and discard any soft onions.

Basic Preparation: To prepare green onions, wash them thoroughly and trim off the roots. Remove any wilted or discolored layers. Green onions may be sliced, chopped, cut into lengths or used whole. The green tops can be cooked, but they cook more quickly than the white bases.

To peel dry onions, slice off the stem and root ends, make a shallow lengthwise slit through the papery skin and remove the outer layer of the onion. To peel pearl onions, drop them into boiling water for about two minutes. Drain the onions and plunge them into cold water to stop the cooking. Cut off the stem end. Squeeze the onions between your thumb and forefinger to separate them from the skins.

To slice dry onions, peel the skin. Cut in half through the root end. Place the onion half, cut side down, on a cutting board. Cut into thin vertical slices. Onions may also be cut crosswise into slices. The slices may be separated into rings. To chop onions, place the cut side down on a cutting board. Cut the onion into slices perpendicular to the root end, holding the onion with your fingers to keep it together. Turn the onion half and cut it crosswise. Repeat with the remaining half.

When onions are cut, they release sulfer compounds that bring tears to the eyes. Try one of these suggestions for minimizing tears:

• Wear glasses or goggles

• Place the onion in the freezer for 20 minutes before chopping.

• Chew a piece of bread while peeling and chopping.

• Chop onions with your mouth closed.

• Work under an exhaust fan.

• Work as quickly as possible, never touching your eyes.

• Wash your hands, knife and cutting surface when finished.

Throughout history, this wonderful little bulb has been hailed for its flavor, pungency and healing powers. Garlic was believed to give courage and strength, to cure diseases such as consumption and influenza and to ward off vampires. Recent studies have shown that eating generous amounts of garlic may play a role in protecting against heart disease. Results indicate that garlic may cause serum cholesterol levels to drop, help prevent blood clots that lead to heart attacks and strokes and aid in lowering blood pressure.

Garlic has been popular for centuries for more than its medicinal qualities! It has found its way into the hearts of millions of people around the world because of its exceptional flavor and versatility. Garlic is a staple in Italian, Chinese, Mexican, Thai and Mediterranean cuisines, just to name a few. Garlic is the star ingredient of buttery shrimp scampi, hearty bowls of chili and crisp Caesar salads.

Garlic Know-How

Although there are many varieties of garlic, most have the same characteristic pungent odor and bite, and they can be used interchangeably in recipes. The most common variety of garlic is American garlic, which has white skin and a strong flavor. Mexican and Italian garlic are pink skinned and taste sweeter. Elephant garlic, with its large cloves, is very mild.

When purchasing garlic, look for heads that are plump, firm to the touch and have no visible damp or brown spots. Garlic will keep anywhere from a few weeks to a few months depending on its age and how it is stored at home. For best results, garlic should be stored in a cool, dark, dry spot.

The whole garlic bulb is called a head. Each individual section is called a clove. Peeling a clove of garlic is very simple—just trim off ends and slightly crush cloves with the flat side of a large knife. The pressure of the knife separates the skin from the clove.

Garlic Tips

There is no need to peel garlic if you are using a garlic press. The garlic gets passed through the press leaving the skin behind. Since pressing garlic releases more of its essential oils, it can be as much as 10 times stronger in flavor as sliced or whole garlic. Keep this in mind when deciding on how much garlic flavor you want in your dish. Don't forget to thoroughly wash your garlic press after each use. The oils left behind in the press can quickly turn rancid and pass an off flavor the next time the press is used.

Roasting garlic produces a mild, sweet, nutty flavor. Because it is milder, roasted garlic can be used more liberally than raw garlic. To roast garlic, simply cut off the top third of the garlic head (not the root end) to expose the cloves; discard the top. Place the head of garlic, trimmed end up, on a 10-inch square of foil. Rub the head generously with olive oil and sprinkle it with salt. Gather thefoil ends together and close tightly. Roast in a preheated 350°F oven 45 minutes or until cloves are golden and the head is soft.

Set aside until cool enough to handle. Gently squeeze the softened garlic head from the root end toward the cut end so that the roasted cloves slip out of their skins into a small bowl. Discard the skins.

Mash the cloves with a fork and use in your favorite recipe. It can also be spread on warm French bread, whipped into mashed potatoes, blended into marinara sauce or used as a sandwich spread. Its uses are endless!

Metric Conversion Chart

VOLUME MEASUREMENTS (dry)

1/8 teaspoon = 0.5 mL
1/4 teaspoon = 1 mL
1/2 teaspoon = 2 mL
3/4 teaspoon = 4 mL
1 teaspoon = 5 mL
1 tablespoon = 15 mL
2 tablespoons = 30 mL
1/4 cup = 60 mL
1/3 cup = 75 mL
1/2 cup = 125 mL
2/3 cup = 150 mL
3/4 cup = 175 mL
1 cup = 250 mL
2 cups = 1 pint = 500 mL
3 cups = 750 mL
4 cups = 1 quart = 1 L

VOLUME MEASUREMENTS (fluid)

1 fluid ounce (2 tablespoons) = 30 mL
4 fluid ounces (1/2 cup) = 125 mL
8 fluid ounces (1 cup) = 250 mL
12 fluid ounces (1 1/2 cups) = 375 mL
16 fluid ounces (2 cups) = 500 mL

WEIGHTS (mass)

1/2 ounce = 15 g
1 ounce = 30 g
3 ounces = 90 g
4 ounces = 120 g
8 ounces = 225 g
10 ounces = 285 g
12 ounces = 360 g
16 ounces = 1 pound = 450 g

DIMENSIONS

1/16 inch = 2 mm
1/8 inch = 3 mm
1/4 inch = 6 mm
1/2 inch = 1.5 cm
3/4 inch = 2 cm
1 inch = 2.5 cm

OVEN TEMPERATURES

250°F = 120°C
275°F = 140°C
300°F = 150°C
325°F = 160°C
350°F = 180°C
375°F = 190°C
400°F = 200°C
425°F = 220°C
450°F = 230°C

BAKING PAN SIZES

Utensil	Size in Inches/Quarts	Metric Volume	Size in Centimeters
Baking or Cake Pan (square or rectangular)	8×8×2	2 L	20×20×5
	9×9×2	2.5 L	23×23×5
	12×8×2	3 L	30×20×5
	13×9×2	3.5 L	33×23×5
Loaf Pan	8×4×3	1.5 L	20×10×7
	9×5×3	2 L	23×13×7
Round Layer Cake Pan	8×1½	1.2 L	20×4
	9×1½	1.5 L	23×4
Pie Plate	8×1¼	750 mL	20×3
	9×1¼	1 L	23×3
Baking Dish or Casserole	1 quart	1 L	—
	1½ quart	1.5 L	—
	2 quart	2 L	—

Acknowledgments

The publisher would like to thank the companies and organizations listed below for the use of their recipes and photographs in this publication.

American Lamb Council

Bertolli U.S.A., Inc.

Birds Eye®

Blue Diamond Growers®

California Olive Industry

California Tomato Commission

California Tree Fruit Agreement

Christopher Ranch Garlic

Colorado Potato Administrative Committee

Del Monte Corporation

Egg Beaters®

Filippo Berio Olive Oil

The Golden Grain Company®

Grey Poupon® Mustard

Hillshire Farm®

Hormel Foods Corporation

Hunt-Wesson, Inc.

The HV Company

Idaho Potato Commission

Kikkoman International Inc.

The Kingsford Products Company

Kraft Foods, Inc.

Land O' Lakes, Inc.

Lawry's® Foods, Inc.

Lipton®

McIlhenny Company (TABASCO® brand Pepper Sauce)

National Onion Association

National Pasta Association

National Pork Producers Council

National Turkey Federation

Newman's Own, Inc.®

Norseland, Inc.

North Dakota Beef Commission

Perdue Farms Incorporated

Reckitt & Colman Inc.

Sonoma® Dried Tomatoes

StarKist® Seafood Company

The Fremont Company, Makers of Frank's & SnowFloss Kraut and Tomato Products

Wisconsin Milk Marketing Board

Index

Index

Index

Index